KNOWING Y

Also by Barry Long

Meditation—A Foundation Course
The Origins of Man and the Universe
Ridding Yourself of Unhappiness
Stillness is the Way
The Myth of Life: cassette series

BARRY LONG

KNOWING YOURSELF

The Barry Long Foundation
London

Published by
The Barry Long Foundation
BCM Box 876 London WC1N 3XX

First published 1983
Reprinted 1984, 1986, 1987, 1988, 1989

© Barry Long 1983

ISBN 0 9508050 1 7

Printed and bound in Great Britain by
Biddles Ltd, Guildford and King's Lynn

This book is about you and it is all true. It contains no theories and no arguments. But you must not believe me for I might be a liar or a fool.

No man can teach another self-knowledge. (Man as I use the word means all of us — woman and man.) He can only lead him or her up to self-discovery — the source of truth. You are either ready to discover yourself or you are not. Ready means you have been knowingly or unknowingly practising self-observation.

This book is an experience in energy. It is not a book about knowing yourself: to read it *is* knowing yourself. If you are ready it is going to disturb you. You are going to feel elevated, excited, confused, uncertain, irritated, resentful, hostile or even physically agitated. All these are normal reactions in different personalities to the energy which is released during the process of knowing yourself. If when you finish reading the book you feel left up in the air, wondering what it was all about or what you should do next to know yourself better, then read it again, and again, and gradually — or in a flash — you'll find the answer.

You don't gather knowledge when you are getting to know yourself — you lose it. Many of your firmest ideas go out the window. You may feel naked, vulnerable, threatened, argumentative, angry. But if you are really looking for the truth and not for some personal vindication you will start to discover you have access to the same source of truth as the wisest teachers who ever lived.

It is a little known fact that truth cannot be memorised. Truth has to be discovered now, from moment to moment. It is always fresh, always new, always there for the still, innocent mind that has experienced life without needing to hold on to what has gone. Truth is of the moment — never of the man.

BARRY LONG

THE PROBLEM

To know yourself completely is to have experienced being God and to have access at any moment to the truth this tremendous experience reveals.

The experience gives the continuous certainty of being responsible for every moment of your life: that whatever happens, the good, the bad and the indifferent, is your own will. Within this all-sustaining knowledge is the unquestionable certainty of immortality, but at the same time it is also possible to experience responsibility for the immediate environment and finally for the entire universe including the earth's apparent discord of war and suffering.

What I have just described is not intellectual possibility but living experience — more intense in its reality and perception than the experience of being alive. But, of course, you must not believe me. You must realise it in yourself, know it, for it is beyond words and thinking. And it has to be experienced without recourse to drugs and insanity. Then you must live your knowledge, be your knowledge. For truth is for all men and women, not just for yourself.

The first barrier to self-knowledge is that man thinks like a machine: we are for or against or switched off, not interested. No-one wants to listen, everyone wants to talk.

We are a world of robot thinkers programmed by robot parents, robot teachers and a robot society. We know little outside what someone else has taught us or said. The little else we think we know we churn out with a monotony that sends us rushing to the television set, the bottle or the record player to drown our own screeching mediocrity.

Every generation of youth seems to sense it and tries to rebel. But to change the robot world we must first change the robot patterns of our own inherited thinking. Revolution without this fundamental change is the substitution of one evil for another — precisely what man has been doing for thousands of years. The young rebels soon put out their wrists contritely to be chained to the rest of the shuffling, mechanical throng.

To be different permanently — and not be a misfit or an eccentric — you must first understand what has to be changed. This is what self-knowledge is all about.

The robot in us is clearly the enemy. It is the cause of most of the worry, suffering and unhappiness in everybody's life. It is the thing we have to understand by becoming conscious — by observing our own mind in action. People are unconscious for most of their lives and they seldom see themselves as they are except by accident. When they do they usually run from the fact in horror. They sleep from birth to death, enmeshed in the robot's thinking which they imagine is themselves.

But, I repeat, you must not believe this. To believe what another says about you is unconscious, robot thinking. Nothing is true in self-discovery unless it is true in your own experience. This is the only protection against the robot levels of the mind.

Truth does not need argument, agreement, theories or beliefs. There is only one test for it and that is to ask yourself "Is the statement true or false in my experience?" The ability to distinguish between true and false depends on your understanding of yourself which in turn depends on how long and how often you are able to remain aware of yourself. Any source claiming to teach you truth or wisdom has to be tested in this way. Truth cannot be taught but it is quickly recognised by the person ready to discover it.

There are two kinds of knowledge. One is worldly knowledge, the knowledge of things outside yourself — what you learned at school, how to drive a car, your work, every activity that makes up the world's and your daily life. This practical side of living gives varying degrees of success, wealth and fame. It produces cleverness, business acumen, lots of words and good advice — but it cannot produce real wisdom.

The other knowledge is self-knowledge — the knowledge of relationships, of fear, desire and all the emotions that make up the me in us.

The robot mind manages to mix these two worlds into an amazingly convincing confusion that leads man nowhere.

If you look at your aims you will find they represent the desire for power, position, prestige, possessions (including people) and permanence (to hold what you have). The desire for success in any of these aspects is really the desire for power.

Everyone pursues them in one form or another in the belief that their fulfilment will result in happiness or contentment. They won't of course, and our terrible inner contradiction is that we secretly realise it.

We know we are only happy for a while no matter what we attain. We are happy with a promotion which gives the prospect of more success in the future, more money now, and immediate prestige. But if we fail to be promoted next time, or have to wait too long, we will be unhappy. Real happiness and contentment if they exist must be a constant, unchanging state that does not depend on the swinging pendulum of success or failure. But everyone keeps chasing the same things because the robot mind cannot pause long enough to look for a source of happiness beyond acquisition.

Are you being told to give up your ambitions, to give up the desire for success, fame and fortune? No. Get out there and acquire the whole world if that is what you want. Out there in the thick of it is the easiest place to discover yourself. No aim, no ambition is too high if you have it. Do not let others infect you with their deadening fear and curb your desire for glory and attainment. Get out there if you can and be one of the few in every generation who clamber above the heads of the masses and wave their hands with a laugh shouting "Look at me world — I made it". But on the way up see you stay conscious, aware of what you are doing. It is the conscious man or woman who finds the secret of happiness and contentment — and that, surely, is the ultimate success.

Self-knowledge reveals rather startling facts. When these are faced you begin to discover what is true and false in the world. If you think you know yourself you are wrong. If you think you know what is true and false in the world you are wrong. Nor do the other four billion or there would be no worry — and everybody worries because everybody thinks the same. To listen, to learn, your mind has to be still.

Have you ever observed that you can have only one thought in your mind at a time? If you are sitting down planning what clothes to take on holiday your mind is on selecting them. If someone asks where you are going that afternoon the holiday planning has to go out of your mind so it can be directed onto the afternoon programme. While you are thinking you cannot listen or absorb anything because your only avenue of awareness is occupied.

If you are told that most of the time you are unconscious it is the habit of the mind to judge immediately and declare: "That is silly. I am conscious. I know I am conscious. If I were unconscious I would not be able to do these things". Can you listen when you judge? Can you learn anything? Or do you only receive your own worn-out opinions, the product of a tiny bit of life you happen to have experienced or read about? But if the response is, "That may be so", you are in a state of receptivity and ready to receive what is new. The still, receptive mind begins with the state of "I do not know so I will listen". The busy, rigid mind begins with "I believe" or "I do not believe" — with judgement and opinions.

The movement each day is for your opinions to grow stronger and more numerous. This is especially true of youth as the robot thinkers gradually sew them up in a cocoon of imagined rights and wrongs and good and bad which all proclaim yet ignore when it suits them — and are insulted if told so.

To break through you have to be in a constant state of listening, for truth is discovered at the most unusual and unexpected times. You have to resist the terrible, crushing, at times almost unbearable pressure of the robot world about you that will do anything — expose you to hate, vilification, tears, ridicule, taunts of insanity, even psychological crucifixion — to make you conform to its way of thinking, get back into line and join the dead who bury the dead.

The pursuit of self-knowledge takes increasing courage. Not the kind of courage that impresses with its daring, but an inner courage that if you have it will eventually give you willpower.

While the mind sees things through opinions and judgements — and it will as long as they are there — you can never see what is true. For example, the belief that God does or does not exist has to be discarded. You don't know. That is the fact. But you can find out through self-knowledge.

The robot minds will try to convince you God does or does not exist, that you should believe even though it is self-evident that you cannot believe anything by an act of will. You have to know to believe, and then you do not have to believe — you know.

Half the world says God exists, the other half disagrees. One of them is wrong. You might believe the wrong one. To believe either is robot thinking because neither knows.

When self-knowledge reveals the answer it will be a living fact in your own experience. At any time you wish to experience the answer it will be there, just as you can say "It is night" or "It is day". You will know while the rest of the world is arguing and speculating.

From this point on you have to discard your opinions of whether another person's behaviour is good or bad. You can judge no-one because you will always perceive them through the slightest distortion of your judgement. Where strong emotion is involved it is not unusual for you to see only your own judgement and not the person at all. And there is always the terrible possibility you might be wrong.

The point of this is that while you are concerned with an opinion about a person you cannot listen and might miss the truth. If someone offends you you can avoid them as much as possible — which you already do anyway — but without thinking about it. Judging someone to another person is this kind of thinking in words. It is the heartbeat of the robot mind.

Everyone has pieces of self-knowledge scattered around their consciousness, unrealised. All it needs is someone to bring them together so that they form a unity, a nucleus to go ahead with.

STARTING OUT

What are you? Every answer to this question comes from the robot mind which lies like a great brick wall between us and the truth. Every answer it gives us about ourselves is but another question, a reaction bouncing back off the same superficial knowledge, an amalgam of what we already know. So we get all the answers but no solutions.

The only way we can ever get through to the truth is by finding out what we are not. We do that by looking, by observation. It is by observing we are not the objects around us that we get our sense of duality, our self-consciousness. So by observing the robot mind in action we gradually disidentify from it and finally realise we are something else. That something — consciousness without the self — is beyond the reactions of the robot and it is there we find the truth.

The robot in us is memory. Worry, fear, every thinking reaction comes out of memory. This must be understood first. You can demonstrate this to yourself now by asking yourself a question — any question — and following what happens.

This process of self-discovery is scientific and the invariable rule of science has to be applied: experiment and observation. The experiment is to ask the question, the observation is to look at yourself and see what happens.

Being a science the laws cannot vary. Any apparent variation is in you: you will have stepped off the way of facts into conclusions.

The sun is either shining or it is not. You do not have to conclude, you just look.

You must forget any theories you have read or heard. We are not concerned with intellectual thinking or arguments here. You do not need to know psychological terms, what Freud said and the rest of it.

When a research scientist enters his laboratory to try to discover something new he leaves outside all his opinions, likes and dislikes. He sets up his experiment, begins the action and observes the results. You have to be a scientist, observing the challenge that life throws up. The beauty of it is that the experiment is always working. You do not have to set aside time or interfere with any of your activities. The hardest part is to make sure the scientist, the observer of yourself, is there.

Sometimes as you peer into the magnificent unexplored depths of yourself your very being will sing at the beauty of a truth discovered and you will exclaim with all the triumph and certainty of a scientist, "It is right". But do not imagine you can share your jubilation with everyone. Unless they are explorers of themselves they will not understand. They may say they do but they cannot, and you will know they do not. The rewards in this process go only to those who make the effort — that is the superb justice of it.

Memory is the product of experience and it contains the facts you use to cope with the practical side of life. But it must also contain something else otherwise we would all agree on the facts and there would be no dispute. You cannot sensibly argue about how many legs a cow has, yet our lives are spent in almost continual dispute and disagreement.

People have wagered their lives on something precarious like their memory of a date. We do it in a smaller way every time we have an argument. People declare with massive all-excluding conviction that such-and-such a thing is true. "I know it is", they cry. Who knows it is? On what immovable ground do these great declarations of truth rest? On impressions.

9

The greatest part of memory consists of impressions. These are the results of conditioning — the religion we were brought up in, our political, family and social environment. It is the most subtle, cloying form of all experience. Impressions are the source of all our opinions and arguments.

Man will give an opinion on almost anything. He does not stop to observe that most of the time he is repeating what someone else has said or written and what he has chosen to believe. He takes other people's ideas as his own or rejects them outright according to his conditioning.

When you say God does or does not exist, or that someone is good or bad, you are drawing on impression memory. When you say you "feel" or "just know" something, you are using impressions. It is unscientific to say you "feel" something. It really means you have not made the effort to find out the fact.

As a child you stopped believing in fairy stories when you found out that magic wands were not a fact of life in your experience. But in the days when you listened to them you were not so sure. You did not have sufficient experience of life to prove them false.

The child does not listen to fairy tales for entertainment or escape. He lives them, and believes them as though they were life itself. The developing mind is so devised that before reading and writing occurred, even before the advent of language, it apprehended all experience in living. With language occurred the first corruption, the first lies and the first fairy tales. So the child continues to believe such things are true until life itself, through his growing up, proves them to be false.

You can make a child believe anything, even that you are magic and wise, but the pose is doomed because life will instruct him by experience that neither is true. Although the child may never find what is true in himself he will discover the fact that you have deceived him and are not wise, and eventually he will not listen to you or consult you. And having failed as a grown-up to find wisdom in himself he will then pretend to his own child that he is wise — with the same tragic results.

The first conditioning we are exposed to, irrespective of community or race, is that we are the body. Then, that we are individuals. Neither can be proved. But we are not going to draw any conclusions, for he who looks and looks long enough must find the truth.

When you next reply "I don't know" to a question, observe the state of no-thought, absence of busy reference to memory, to conditioning and impressions. You are like a photographic plate exposed in a darkroom, absolutely still yet perfectly poised to receive the light, the new.

You do not have to find what is true: when the false is discarded truth is there.

FACING THE FACT

Self-knowledge is the process of becoming de-hypnotised. When you are hypnotised you see things as they really are not, mistaking the false for the true. A self-deluding process is required — a robot imagination.

Without imagination man would not be man. Yet it is the main obstacle to self-knowledge. The trouble begins when we allow imagination to use us, and this occurs whenever it draws its images out of impression memory and not factual memory. Then we suffer. And if we use our misery to observe ourselves we discover that this type of imagination is the curse of man — the thing that separates us from God, if there is a God.

Things get done through factual memory. Through it the world progresses materially. From medicine to space-ships, every new device and practical service to mankind has its origin as a progressive development of factual memory. Man always uses it in his work or when there is something important to do. But as soon as he finishes work he switches over to impression memory — emotional memory. This is where he keeps his imaginings of the significance of experience, of what he is and what others are. Here he is no longer concerned with facts. He enters the world of imagination and opinions — the world of the false. Yet when he had an important job to do, when he could not afford to fail, he dealt only in facts.

Countless men and women have each contributed in their own way to progress but have not contributed one fact to answer the question "Where am I going — what is it all about?". Are the ones who came before you your hypnotists? Are you in turn the hypnotist of your children? There is only one way to find out. You have to see yourself exactly as you are, not as you imagine you are.

When you observe yourself you must not condemn or approve what you see. If you tell a lie there is no need to judge yourself. The judge cannot be the judged, and even to accept is to judge. The fact is that you lied — there is no need to tell anyone else, just face the truth alone.

As you continue watching yourself you will observe you are an habitual liar. Even if you are recounting a simple happening you will observe yourself lie or exaggerate for no reason. If you try to find a reason you are judging again, trying to justify. You will be amazed at what you see. The scientist when he is observing the results of an experiment is often amazed at what he sees, and he can laugh at it too without changing the result.

If you try to change what you see you have failed again. To succeed in any endeavour you have to keep coming back to your object. Your object is to see yourself exactly as you are. You are not just a liar, you are many other disagreeable things. If you try to change them all you will not have time to know yourself. You will neither know yourself nor change yourself and you will be back with all the others before you who tried to change themselves and never succeeded.

If we could change things easily by opposition what a mess we would be in. What is good to some is bad to others. Some would change the good, others would change the bad. There is no escape from the old in the old or we would all be free. Self-knowledge is the discovery of the new: it looks beyond the world that has all the answers and no solutions.

A woman (or man) buys a diamond ring. It costs a lot of money and for two years she wears it with the satisfaction that can go with owning something beautiful or valuable. One day an expert proves that it is a worthless imitation. Does she continue to wear it? No. She throws it away or gives it to her children to play with.

The truth is that once you discover something is false you lose interest in it. Man no longer treasures what he thought genuine once he discovers it is false. In this way truth is its own solution.

Self-knowledge is the discovery of the false. You do not have to find what is true: when the false is discarded truth is there. It always was. Just keep observing the fact and the change will come automatically and will be lasting. When you discover you are a liar and face the fact without excuses you will begin to stop lying. Lying will drop away like the dead leaf that is no longer part of the tree.

You are also a hypocrite. You are cruel, selfish, greedy and envious. You do not live up to the standards of behaviour and thought you profess and expect of others. You allow yourself the indulgence of anger but condemn it in others. You will cheat in a business deal and excuse it as business, talk about and defame another man or woman to amuse yourself in conversation and then go home and say you love. If this is love there is no hope. Love, if it exists, must be a constant thing and not the plaything of inconstancy.

Life is a stream sweeping you along and the facts are like immovable rocks in the middle of the stream. Face each fact as it presents itself and rest — and the stream will carry you around and beyond. Struggle away from the fact by not facing it and you fight against the stream of life and suffer. It is the law. There is no other way.

To face a fact is to look at it full on, no matter how ugly or painful it is. Then it dissolves and like the smashed atom releases a tremendous energy which we apprehend as the moment of decision or the moment of truth.

If a man wants to find out what is in a valley over the hill he climbs to the top of the ridge and looks. He does not say the river at the north end should be at the south. He does not say what should be and what should not be. He looks. He sees first only what is — the valley and all that is in it — as it is. If he now desires to live in the valley things can be changed if they are changeable. The fact that they are changeable will change them though — the man will merely be the instrument. His desire to live in the valley is not the fact. It is only the path leading up to the fact.

If the river is too far away to water his land and cannot be diverted the man will have to face the fact, perhaps even weep at the frustration of his desire, and go elsewhere. If the river can be changed he will face the fact and divert it. He does not have to judge anything as long as he keeps facing facts.

The fact comes first. It is always that way, but it cannot be seen unless the mind is very still. At first it is seen as a glimpse but the insight will return, stronger, when you have worked more.

The opposite, the lingering misery of living, would occur if the man did not face the fact of no water and moved into the valley on the strength of his desiring and its blind optimism. That would be imagination, dreamland with reality's agony.

Why is it that most magazines devote the front page to a picture of a pretty girl although she may not be connected with the contents? And she is always smiling, looking happy or sexy.

The answer is obvious to the robot mind but it is still not understood. If everyone understood it the advertisements would not work. But the fact is that the manufacturers and advertising men who deal in these things know the treatment pulls. The aim is to create desire for the objects by planting an alluring impression in your mind that happiness comes from using or owning these things.

This one-sided presentation works because happiness and contentment are not known. If they were, any attempt even to suggest that something can produce them when it does not would be ridiculous. It would be like trying to convince you a feather is the cause of happiness because when someone is tickled with it it makes them laugh. Laughter is not the indicator of happiness, as we all know.

People imagine happiness is associated with possessions, whether money, houses, cars, television sets, pretty girls or handsome men. They never cease imagining this even though in their own experience the happiness of possession inevitably wilts and droops. So the false is tolerated and believed because the fact is not faced and is therefore powerless to bring the new.

Our object here is to discover what is false. By observation we have discovered that imagination is false when it separates the part from the whole and builds on only one aspect of a fact — an impression. So if you separate yourself from this imagining you separate yourself from the false. If you identify with it you identify with the false and you are unconscious, robot thinking. When you are identified with a state you are that state. When you are angry you are anger. When your thinking is unreal so are you.

You can never stop anger by a decision. Anger is the same monster every time. Its energy is emotion and emotion is the result of conflict. Conflict comes from robot imagining and that is the result of trying to change what is without facing the fact.

Anger, like all the other corrupting identities in you, has to be observed and understood and then it disintegrates and never returns. You cannot be anger and the observer at the same time, but you can appear to be angry and still be the observer. It takes tremendous power to remain the observer under provocation. But anger, being false, cannot exist in the spotlight of intelligent observation.

☆

The truth, which is the real good, can be discovered first only in relation to yourself. To do this the mind has to be very still. But to see the truth or what is good for other people requires a great amount of work on yourself.

Stored away in your impression memory is what you imagine to be good for you and the various people in your life, for humanity, for the world and all things generally. But you do not even know the truth in relation to yourself yet. To see the truth in relation to someone else is absolutely beyond your capability. So our attempts to live together are a constant collision of everyone's imaginings of what everyone's needs are. You do not know the fact about yourself or them and they do not know the fact about themselves or you. What a circus.

"Why can't I find happiness?", man asks. "Why are there quarrels, greed, murder, suicides, wars? Why can't people live together in harmony? Why am I never really content, no matter what I acquire, whether it be man or woman, gold or power?"

It is quite simple. You do not know your need, and you will never know it unless you know yourself. You see all needs through the eyes of the ephemeral robot, not understanding that the purpose of need is the need of life to experience itself as a totality beyond the apparent individual needs of men and things. So there is the mystery of death and destruction and birth and life — a structural justice, an integrity of opposites, a being of all things called immortal life.

You still imagine another's need as do the do-gooders — and that includes all of us at some time — and the professional reformers. The latter will reform anything except themselves. The do-gooder and the professional reformer never solve anything. They work on the outside on what appears to be a need. They deal in appearances, not understanding that every appearance is an expression of a cause beyond itself. They relieve a pocket of poverty in the mighty garment of the world but only for a moment in the majesty of its years. Everything they touch falls back to what it was when they discover a more "needy" cause. They sometimes leave bitterness and misery behind, for those they fed hunger again and those they saved fall again. They have given of their time, perhaps of their possessions, but not of themselves. You cannot give what you do not know, or you are not the giver. And what is it to give of your possessions? One day you may lose them and you will have nothing to give.

B e still and know that you are love.

LOVE

For the moment you must forget anything you ever thought you knew about love. If you look through the screen of the old you cannot understand and you will not be listening.

You cannot love a person, a thing or an event. But you can be in the state of love in relation to it. Then you are the object's need or it is your need, and your love will continue — but only as long as the need lasts.

If the object does not or cannot know itself, it might not consciously recognise its love. An example of this is the air you breathe. It is in a state of love in relation to you. It is your need and without it you will die. But you are not consciously in a state of love with it; when you know yourself you will be. Just now someone has to put a pillow over your head for you to see your love — air. When they remove the pillow you go back to sleep — which you call living — oblivious of the delight of knowing this love. You are alive according to your knowledge of love.

Love is choiceless, just as the air has no choice but to support your life and you have no choice but to breathe it. A real reformer is a person in love. He has no choice, he acts because he cannot do otherwise.

The mind draws only on the past, on your experience and on the experience of others which is stored in memory, books or records of some kind. Any product of the mind is a reaction of the past, a synthesis of what is old. So mind is a modifier, a reactor, a renovator, but it cannot create the new.

In the state of love you have to be creative: you have no choice — and you want none. Love is beyond description but not beyond demonstrating. It is beyond the mind because it is always new. The mind cannot know love. Where there is thought, love is not. Awareness can know love because you can only experience the new when you are aware, when you are thought-less. We are, however, seldom still enough to know what we love, especially in relation to the work we do. Even if we knew we would probably choose the career that seemed to promise success and money. Thus in our jobs we are mostly unhappy or only reasonably happy — which means dissatisfied — and we are mostly mediocre and uncreative in them.

When the robot mind is active it thinks all the time and is the master. When the robot mind is mastered, undisciplined thinking ceases and is replaced by awareness. When the leading architects of the world, the most original designers, the most gifted writers create, their minds are in a state of meditation — or stillness — on their "love".

And out of the silence, the beyond, into the silent waiting mind comes the fulfilment of the need, the fact, the refreshing new that sets the rest of the poor, mediocre, thinking world agog with its brilliance and genius.

Man's needs are ever being filled, therefore ever changing. When a need is filled there is no longer any need. That is why love as we know it never seems to last. It is not the love that changes, it is the need.

It is the action of the mind to cling to what it has known even though the fact is that there is no need. The mind imagines that love is for ever as it has read and heard and wants so much to create — and never can.

Love is for ever, invariable and changeless, but not in relation to any object. For all things have a need and when that need is satisfied the love that provides it must change and appear as another need.

Love's movement is always towards union. It is the unifier of creation, the destroyer of division. The final need is love itself. So if you loved something as your one remaining need you would have to die. Not die for — which is the robot mind's imagination of the ultimate in love — but die into. Then you would be one — no lover, no beloved.

You can only give as much as you understand.

GIVING

If you look at life's totality you will notice that everything exists for something else. Everything is like a tunnel: at one end it receives and at the other end it gives. In between it converts what it receives into a suitable form for the thing above or below to receive. This is not a giving or receiving by choice, it is choiceless. There has to be giving as there has to be receiving. Death, preceded by unconsciousness, is the terminator for the failure to give and receive.

Why is it that so often when you give to another with a generous smile and gesture you at the same time feel the stab of selfishness and know you really do not want to give? Why is it that when someone gives to you you often notice your torrent of thanks does not carry the sincerity you verbally express? That for a strange, almost frightening reason you are not moved at all and could just as easily take and walk away?

You have to receive what you need under the unbreakable law of the universe, and what you need is not what you imagine you need. Here is the tide that knows no individual. The mind will always come up with a reason why you gave or received. It will say you wanted to or that you were a fool to give and won't do it again. But in the massive sweep of life the fact remains that you had no choice.

When your mind imagines what you need or imagines that you are giving out of choice, at that moment you can experience in yourself the lie of hypocrisy. For that moment — if you see it — you are conscious.

You go through the act of gratitude because your mind says "everyone would be grateful in the same position". Gratitude is, but it is beyond the robot mind although not beyond experiencing. It is a state that can only exist when the giver gives because he would die if he did not and the receiver receives because he would die if he did not. In the moment neither thinks and neither speaks and neither feels he is the giver or the taker, and the experience is sacred because in the moment both receive love.

All life begins with the sun. The sun shines and gives of itself: it has no choice. Heat from the sun evaporates water, clouds build up and when they become too heavy it rains and they give of themselves. The air must give of itself to man's body as breath, and man in breathing converts the oxygen to carbon dioxide to give it to the trees so that they can breathe their need and in living convert it back to oxygen so that man's body may breathe again. The earth must give of itself to the trees and grass and they give of themselves to the animals and birds who give of themselves to man. And when all things die they must go back to feed the earth and the earth receives and gives so all things can receive and give — none has a choice.

But all this is unconscious giving and receiving. Of all created things, man alone possesses the potential to give the thing that all creation is waiting for, the thing that only man can give: consciousness. To give consciousness is simply a matter of becoming conscious, waking up. When man by rediscovering the truth of choicelessness begins to know himself he begins to become conscious, to wake up, and he begins to give.

But although he has received and possesses the capability to give the most precious gift, the final need of all creation — consciousness — he does not give it. He chooses not to; and so he perpetuates selfishness and ignorance on the planet by contributing nothing through his life except to himself.

Life's penalty for not giving or receiving consciously is unconsciousness. So man like all things is unconscious. Unconsciousness is the next to last need of all things with a brain, and death is the final need of all unconscious life. So all unconscious life, including man the way he is, is mortal.

Man conscious is man immortal. Man conscious gives to the creation as no other thing can give and is beyond death which is the final need of all things unconscious. But it is no use my just saying this. You must discover it, realise it for yourself.

When death comes there is no time. We always imagine we will die to-morrow. But when we die we die today.

MARS!

In Eastern countries, especially in India, people pay a lot of attention to astrology. Astrology is studied as a predictive science: they believe that the nine planets which revolve with the earth around the sun govern the lives of everyone and that the future can be foretold from the positions they will occupy. Astrologers have made some amazingly accurate predictions and countless blunders.

We are not concerned with astrology, but astrology contains a principle we can use in the study of ourselves.

According to astrology each planet possesses certain characteristics that cause specific events in people's lives. We will look at only three planets. Mars, the astrologers say, is a fiery energetic planet which causes accidents, violence, fire, blood, hate, war and anger. Mars is quick and hurts like a punch on the nose. Saturn is a slow-moving planet that causes misery, sorrow, poverty, sullenness and delay. Jupiter is the great giver of good, according to astrology. We will look at it later.

Round and round the planets go and because they are at a certain point in relation to their position when you were born so you hit your thumb with a hammer, get off on the wrong foot with your new boss, no longer make progress despite increased efforts, win a lottery or get a pay rise.

Let us now forget astrology and look at life in relation to the Mars and Saturn elements.

Very few, if any, of the things we attempt go according to our expectations. Not only big things but everything. The things that go wrong are the Mars and Saturn elements in life. We will refer to them from now on as the Mars element. The robot mind treats these things as separate from life, as unconnected happenings that interfere with or spoil the enjoyment of living. They are bad luck, bad news, a sad event, a cruel blow, a setback. They cause worry, tears, anger, rejection, fear, discontent — most of the feelings that are the opposite to the feelings of happiness and contentment.

What we are leading up to is a device to help you keep awake, conscious, while the robot minds around you snore on, imagining they know. But remember the mind will fight you all the way — with judgements and opinions about what is being said — and if you give in you will be unconscious again.

If the Mars element were absent you would merely desire something and it would be yours. There would be no interference, no competition, nothing to overcome, nothing to deflect you, no sorrow, no challenge, no disappointment, no accidents, no hospitals, no pain, no debt, no death.

Do you see the absurdity of this division? Follow its thinking through and you mentally destroy the fact of life and create what must be paradise. But life is the fact — or would you deny it?

Whenever the Mars element strikes you are upset to varying degrees. Whenever it appears to be absent you are happy or undisturbed. If the Mars element were absent forever and everything went smoothly you would imagine that that would be the secret of happiness and contentment. Obviously it is, but as we have seen, to experience this state we would destroy living as the intelligent mind knows it. Unless — and this is the only alternative — unless you could accept everything that happened as a part of life and did not react to it. That would be the practical secret of happiness and contentment.

The robot mind pursues everything it sets out to do with the attitude that there will be no interference from the Mars element, that life will actually suspend the essence which is its existence. You might say that people expect things to go wrong. That is saying something and not living it. If you expected things to go wrong or differently, if you had a mental attitude that acknowledged the ever-present possibility of Mars, you could never get angry or upset when it struck.

You get in a friend's car and smash the wing as you drive up the street. Your reaction is a degree of worry, anguish or fear. You are shocked when Mars strikes, otherwise you would have no reaction. Look at it closely but do not look for contradictions. If you see this main fact the side issues that your mind wants to raise will become clear. The mind is your greatest enemy. Its very function is to keep the truth hidden. You smash the car and suffer worry. But if you were conscious of the fact that the Mars element is there you could not worry. To worry or suffer mentally about the fact of life is ridiculous. Why not worry about all the other people who will smash their cars today, who will lose a limb, the children who will be crippled, the fifty thousand who will die of starvation? Why not worry about all the rest of life that life itself will afflict today? You cannot worry about them, can you? It is impossible.

Worry is a purely selfish expression. The fact is that to worry or suffer mentally you have to have an opinion. You have to say "that is bad in relation to me". That opinion will prevent you from seeing the truth. When you smash the car the only fact in your experience is that the car is smashed. It is your judgement that it is bad. Most people, you might say, especially the owner, will agree with you that it is bad.

No they will not. The smash will be good for the man who repairs the car and for those he employs: without car-smashes and breakdowns they would be out of work. It will be good for the company who make the spare parts and if the car is a write-off it will be good for the car manufacturers and all the people who work for them. You may imagine it is bad for the insurance company but it will be good for the bank which provides the insurance company's overdraft at a profit out of which it pays wages. It will be good for the typewriter and stationery people and the post office because it will involve letters, documents, stamps and phone calls, and so on. In fact it appears to be bad only for the owner, the insurance company and you. But the insurance company exists because of the profits it makes on such risks and if there were no accidents there would be no insurance companies. So it is not bad for the company. For the owner, the smash is the Mars element, which is life, and he judges that life is bad because the smash is bad for him. If he would eliminate Mars from his life it must be eliminated from all lives and that, as you have seen, would be the end of life. Everyone you know wants to eliminate the bad from their lives.

Life is composed of the coming and going of money. What money is spent on does not matter. The bloodstream of your life is the coming and going of money. Some things like smashes do seem unnecessary but this is because you live on the surface. Has anyone ever succeeded in avoiding such things?

The movement of money is a total act of life and not of the individual. It is like the tide — it sweeps in and out leaving behind numberless small puddles of various sizes and capacities which it will destroy or refill at will when it flows in again. All of life depends on this constant regular movement, and the mass of little puddles which make up the container of the full tide must give back continuously so that the puddles on the other side of life can be refreshed — and the bigger life maintained.

The only reason the smash is bad for you is because you fear what the owner will say or think about you and you do not like the Mars element in your life of being blamed and feeling guilty. So it is not really bad for you except in your imagination. To fear what the owner will say or to feel uncomfortable you will have to separate that which is life from your life. This can only be done in imagination. Worry exists only in relation to you, the individual, and you can observe that the thing which gives you the greatest pleasure will give you the greatest pain. To dodge the Mars element — which is life — you will have to die.

Do you see the stupidity of being surprised when life hits you? Only death can save you, but you, the robot mind, regard the inescapable fact of death as the worst blow of life.

Death is all that life is: a continuous trauma that produces understanding.

WAKING UP

To wake up, to see yourself and all things as they are and not as you imagine them to be, you need a shock. There has to be something to keep disturbing you. At present you will find it impossible to stay conscious for longer than a second or two at a time. It is a tremendous effort in the beginning to see yourself seeing what you are seeing. The drag of unconscious sleep will overtake you just as ordinary sleep pulls at the lids and overtakes the exhausted man.

The Mars element in life will never let you down. It will shock you every time. Whenever Mars strikes say to yourself "Mars!" and observe your reaction. If you just cry "Mars!" and do not look at yourself reacting to the event you are wasting your time. If you do not see what responds at the moment of challenge how can you know what you are?

In the beginning you will have to rely on Mars, but if you can remember to observe yourself when Mars is not hitting that is very good. But you must never condemn, approve or judge your reaction. It is vitally important that you just observe. You will find you cannot live with a fool once you see he is a fool.

An unconscious man separates the Mars element from his life by judging it as bad in relation to him. This creates conflict or friction — his judgement that it should not have happened to him against the fact of life that it did happen. The conflict or friction between what is and man's idea of what should be generates emotion, and this emotion is the energy that powers temper. The same Mars situation happens to two men. One is unmoved inwardly, there-fore conscious of all about him and able to take any intelligent action that might be needed. The other is a raging machine, quite unconscious because he can have only one thought at a time and his mind is aflame with exploding or simmering emotion. He is incapable of intelligent action and himself becomes a potential instrument of the Mars element.

The Jupiter element is the opposite to the Mars element. It is good luck, the fortunate occurrence, success, the unexpected win, the end of delay, the miraculous escape and so on. But strangely, good fortune is like an injection of morphine — it puts you into a deeper sleep. That is why a man once said it is easier for a camel to pass through the eye of a needle than for a rich man to enter the kingdom of heaven. A rich man has too much to lose before he really suffers and turns inward. As you become conscious you will be able to see Jupiter as you see Mars. It is a Mars situation when a plate slips out of your hand, and a Jupiter one when you catch the plate an inch from the ground.

The Mars element is pain and there is no mystery about pain, mental or physical: its purpose is to drive you towards awareness, to wake you up. If you see this, pain has a purpose, otherwise you suffer for nothing.

The state of awareness is the state in which you see things as they are; the precious facility that life has given man to escape the mastery of the robot. It is the habit of the mind to destroy as quickly as possible the state of awareness. It does this by judging, for judging is thinking.

If you want to see what is inside a room you open the door and look in. To see everything exactly as it is you have to be in a state of awareness, in the mental attitude of listening, and this state is possible only when you are not thinking. You can only see things as they are when you do not think.

All your opinions, dislikes and most of your likes come out of memory. They are the result of some personal experience in the past or have been gained through reading, hearing, being influenced or conditioned.

But you cannot know what you have not experienced, and what you have experienced is all past. Every moment is new. If it were not you could tell the future by the past. If you look at what is new through the screen of the past — your opinions — it is no longer new.

If you say you do not like the type of table in the room there are two possibilities. One is that it resembles a table you have seen in the past and stored as an unpleasant image in your memory. The second is that it is in some way new in your experience. It is the habit of the robot mind to reject the new. The mind hates change and you will always resist the new if it conflicts with your opinions, especially with what you imagine your interests to be.

Quite often you find that the new leaves you rather indifferent and it is difficult to decide whether you like it or not. You find this embarrassing at times because you cannot form an opinion, and everyone is expected by the intelligent robot mind to have opinions. But after your mind gets used to the sight of the new, such as the design of a new car or a new look in clothes, you will probably find yourself saying you like it — or you will make up or steal an opinion.

Before introducing a new look experienced designers and manufacturers condition the public robot mind by publishing photographs and impressions as widely as possible. In politics also they seldom move without conditioning through a leaked newspaper or magazine story before introducing the new.

So if you say you do not like a table your opinion is based either on the past or on the habit of the mind — which is mechanical. Neither is an intelligent state. Dislike is a judgement of the robot and a negative interpretation of the natural state of preference. Preference, being the natural state, does not require thinking and that is why you like things without knowing why. What you mean when you say you do not like the table is that you would not choose it for yourself, you would prefer another. But it is not your moment to choose: you are judging someone else's moment, their preference of table, and by doing that you divide yourself from them and division is disharmony.

When it is your moment to do the choosing you do not dislike tables you do not choose. You just choose the one you prefer, and in that moment you are aware — and your choice is choiceless.

Your choice is vanity.

THE MOMENT

Man is not as complex as he often thinks he is — with a glimmering of satisfaction. He is complex in the sense that a tin of worms is complex. To the observer it is just a tin of worms. What the tin of worms is doing might be complex to the worms but the observer can tell without looking that they are wriggling and squiggling like a tin of worms.

There is only one thing in your life you can be sure of. That one thing is this moment, now. The last moment has gone forever. The next moment has not come. It is an inescapable fact that only the moment, now, exists in relation to you. The future exists only in your imagination and that is why, no matter how hard you try to imagine it, you will not be able to tell the future.

You can become fully conscious only when you are living in the moment. To begin to live in the moment you have to know it exists and understand it. To understand it you have to observe it in relation to yourself and in relation to life. When you understand it, when you become conscious, you will see it is all that exists. To see this is to glimpse reality.

Everything that happens to you — the good, the bad and the indifferent — happens in the moment. It is the mind's interpretation of the moment through an old impression that keeps you asleep. The moment occurs in your experience as a happening which is the fact. In the next moment your mind re-acts through a stored impression by responding to the happening as thought. You are then living in the past, hanging on to a moment that has gone. The moment, the new in life, is passing every moment, but by clinging to an old moment as an impression of this moment your mind keeps you unconscious of the only thing that exists for you.

The secret is that the moment is perfect. Thinking is the imperfection and is unnecessary. The more you observe life in relation to yourself the more you will see the fact that you are hardly ever correct when you think by predicting the gloom of the future, becoming angry, doubting or being fearful.

Irritation at having to do something in the future is the jarring vibration of having put the moment out of place: you mistake the disharmony you feel now for the imagined future bother. The strange fact is that nothing is tedious or unpleasant at the moment of doing it unless you think.

But how do you plan for the future if you do not think? You plan by looking, not thinking. If you think, you are using your emotional or impression memory — the beginning of confusion, worry and wishful thinking. When you plan you use factual memory, not impression memory. You plan by looking at the relevant facts of your experience and the looking itself reveals everything you need to know, moment to moment.

For example, to remember the things you own all you have to do is direct your attention onto them and then, without thinking, up they come, one by one. You cannot remember all you own at the same moment. The process is to ask yourself "What do I own?". Your mind is temporarily stilled and up out of memory comes one object followed by another and another until the line runs out.

In planning, if any facts you need are missing you obtain them by action; then you look again. Once you have made a decision or find you cannot proceed further you drop the subject from your consciousness and there is no thinking or worrying. You just stay aware and look from time to time to see if there has been any change in the situation.

Only one conscious action can exist at any one moment for any one individual. It is impossible for life to make two conscious demands of you at once. One will be imagination—your impression of what you should be doing. The moment is your only duty. Or to answer a question that bothers some, the moment is God's will.

Your duty at any time in your life is to do what you have to do from moment to moment. What you have to do is what you cannot avoid doing. What you cannot avoid doing is what you do. Life is not interested in the reasons your mind produces — the reason might or might not be correct, but the fact is always correct and the fact is that you do it. The moment and not the anticipation of the moment is perfect.

You will do thoughtless, stupid, cruel, dishonest things. Afterwards either you yourself or someone else will label the action in words for you, and you mentally suffer. You ask yourself how you could have done such a thing, but the fact is you did it. Life reveals itself only to the conscious. It is only because you are a machine that you suffer, and the purpose of suffering is to wake you up.

Sometimes you will find yourself looking full on at the Mars element in your life which is always from your point of view the apparent disharmony of two moments. What you call disharmony is not disharmony to life. The disharmony of course is in the robot mind's desire to control life according to its individual interests: an impossibility — but you will keep trying.

We can rarely see things from the point of view of another person because we look at the fact through the screen of an impression or an interest which distorts our view — and there are accusations, quarrels and misunderstanding.

If you use the moment of being rebuked or blamed to observe your reaction you will become more conscious. You will observe yourself making an excuse, giving a reason. You will make the excuse because you do not like being blamed and man, being a machine whose direction can be easily predicted, always trots out an excuse. If the evidence is overwhelming and he can offer no explanation he will quickly find someone to tell the story to with wrong emphasis and with lies so that the listener will have to agree he was justified in his action.

Each moment provides a challenge to you to become conscious. All things and all possibilities exist in the creation. You might meet someone, there might be a rain storm, sudden pain, a letter, you might lose something — this is the moment's world. No-one can ever know what it will throw up because no-one can ever know all it contains. The game is to be waiting — and aware.

Man thinks there is individuality of mind but there is not. Mind always operates the same. When you know yourself you know all minds.

THE MAN MACHINE

A machine always functions in a pre-determined way. You can predict exactly what a machine will do if you have sufficient knowledge of it. A machine cannot go beyond the limitations of its design. It can stop, or run inefficiently, but it cannot of itself change the pattern of its function.

Trees and plants have different appearances but they all use the same mechanical process and their performance, according to your knowledge of the plant machine, can be predicted. Even a layman can predict that they will absorb sustenance through a root system, form branches and produce flowers, fruit or leaves.

The cow machine will give milk if it is fed, will produce young in a certain time if mated, will run away from an outside cause of pain, will attack you if you threaten its young. Similarly, with small variations, the dog machine, the elephant machine, the water machine, the light machine, the sound machine, the sun machine, the moon machine, the earth machine — the performance of all can be predicted according to your knowledge of the machine after making allowance for the Mars element.

The direction the man machine will always take is one of the easiest to predict. He will devote his life to the desire for money, power, prestige and if he possesses any of these things and loses them he will be unhappy.

If he thinks he is going to lose any of them he will worry.

If any of his desires are fulfilled he will be happy, but only while he is thinking about or experiencing the fulfilment. Otherwise he will be discontented or restless because of the non-fulfilment of his other desires.

Like the animal and insect machines he (and especially she) will protect the young even to death, and imagine that his love is above the love of all the other animal and insect machines that do the same thing without an act of will which is what man says motivates him.

The man machine will always somehow give preference to his own young over another's and say it is natural, not understanding that what is natural is mechanical.

He imagines he possesses dignity and will go to the most un-dignified lengths to prove it, being unable to understand that what possesses dignity does not need to prove it — cannot lose it.

He will crucify any conscious man who tries to help him, and finally convert the man's wisdom into an empty, mechanical dogma that suits his understanding.

He will espouse a code of ethical behaviour based on the teaching of a man who was not a machine, and will observe none of it because a machine cannot change its function or understand what is true.

The man machine will imagine attachment to be love, so each one is baffled by the exhortation to love one another. The young, while being made into machines by the others' example and training, ask "How do you love one another?" because they have seen it to be unnatural in themselves and that no-one else does — and are further machine-ised by imaginative answers and excuses.

The man machine will fear death because a machine cannot see beyond its own destruction. He will also mourn the death of others — but only the death of those to whom he is attached — as though it were some unexpected event in life.

What are you — a body, a mind? While you accept these limitations you remain those things and they become your environment. The interaction between them is what you call circumstances. Man must rise above circumstances.

CONSCIOUSNESS

If you are only the body there is no hope of life after death, reincarnation or heaven, and Christ, Buddha, Abraham and all the prophets were fools. Yet if you are not the body, what are you?

Your body is yours. Pinch it and it hurts. Pinch someone else and you feel nothing. But that does not necessarily mean your body is you. It could be an expression of you as the note is an expression of the bell. When the note has died the bell still is. So your body is yours but not necessarily you.

If there is no desire to eat or breathe the body rots and vanishes. Remove desire and the body does not exist. So the body exists because of desire — but whose desire?

When you are asleep you are unconscious — you are absent. You exist only because you wake up and regain consciousness. While you are asleep and absent the body must breathe because it is alive when you wake up. It is not your desire that makes the body breathe. Even when you are awake it is not your desire that keeps the body breathing. You only appear and act when the body's breathing is impaired. So it is the body's desire to breathe.

It must be the body's desire to eat too. You do not decide you are hungry. You become aware of discomfort in the body and after the sensation you realise you are hungry. In the same way you feel well or sick, hot or cold. You do not decide any of these things.

You always appear after the sensation and then decide the action. So you cannot be the body.

You are what you believe you are. But you probably cannot say what you believe you are. You can only say what you imagine you believe you are.

The truth, as always, lies in the source of all truth — life. What you believe, you live, or you do not believe it. Your beliefs can never be separated from your daily life and what you parade as your beliefs in discussion and argument is what you imagine you believe.

In the first instance man believes he is the body, and according to that belief he lives, enjoys and suffers. It is all identification — only this time it actually dictates his life and destiny. How is this possible?

Everything has consciousness because everything has knowledge. Where there is no knowledge there is no thing, and unless there is a knower — consciousness — there is no knowing and no knowledge.

To exist, a thing must first possess the knowledge to function as itself. If consciousness has only the knowledge of a worm it appears as a worm; if it has the knowledge of a dog, as a dog. While it has only the knowledge of a worm it will always behave like a worm. As consciousness knows so it appears and behaves. The study of the behaviour of a thing is the study of its knowledge. If we can find out what it knows we can predict its behaviour, and that is exactly what the scientist does.

Man is the only thing that possesses the capability of knowing its own knowledge or its function. To know your function is to know yourself. Man seldom knows himself, but he like all things has degrees of self-knowledge. The degree is the thing's knowledge which appears as its function or behaviour.

Now we can see why man lives what he believes. He functions according to his knowledge of himself. If he does not know his

49

knowledge or his function he is not conscious and he does not know himself.

If you are not conscious it means you do not know what you know. To be conscious is to be consciousness: the knower, the supporter of all knowledge. The knower in you, which is consciousness, cannot be the known, for knowledge varies but consciousness cannot. Although consciousness cannot be known it can be experienced. You can experience consciousness now by experiencing the fact that you exist. The difference between this and any other experience is that it is done independently of any state or thing. It is the only completely independent action man is capable of. In this brief moment you will notice you do not have to know anything. You do not even have to know you exist. You just are, or as you would say yourself, "I am".

You cannot hold that state because you start to think. Not about anything in particular, but your mind runs off on an association prompted from outside by one of your senses. So you think, you become that thought, and consciousness, the state of pure awareness, is lost.

It is the way of things in this creation that every condition is the opposite of another. There is hot and cold, high and low, birth and death, pure and impure, gross and refined and so on. The movement of life where it can be distinguished always seems to be from the gross to the refined, from the impure to the pure. This eternal, seldom-apprehended progression is what man knows as hope.

Knowledge follows this law. At one end it is gross, at the other refined. The lower end in relation to existence might be the knowledge possessed by a stone. In relation to man the lower end might be the knowledge of a brute, the higher end the knowledge of a Christ.

There are two links between man's consciousness and his knowledge. Reason links him with factual memory. Imagination links him with impression memory. The highest knowledge man can possess is that which is true in his own experience. If his experience is limited, so is his knowledge and he behaves accordingly. A brute of a man cannot have had the same experience as a Christ. But a Christ must have had the same experience as a brute or there is no progression. The highest knowledge must be the most reliable too, or the law breaks down.

If someone tells you it is raining and you look around and see it is not you say it is not. It does not matter what authority the person has, he cannot convince you otherwise because in your own experience at that moment you know the fact. You know it in the same way as you know you exist, and that is the supreme certainty of all experience.

The faculty you have used is reason. Reason first uses the facts of the individual's own experience. As it moves away from that living moment into the experience of others it becomes imagination, and the likelihood of error is increased enormously. For reason is only the Christ end of the brute imagination.

To know something in your own experience, just as you know you exist, does not require imagination. All you have to do is observe. You need no outside knowledge, no techniques, no talents as the world applauds them, no authority, no university degree, no books, no assistance. It is the simple, beautiful experience of aloneness — which is the opposite of loneliness.

The fact is always simple. The difficulty is in seeing it through the mind which until it is stilled always takes the imaginative way. The mind knows it is the master in imagination and the slave of the fact. It will fight you all the way to self-knowledge — and why not? It is the only enemy.

We have seen that hunger and breathing are desires of the body. It is obvious from man's behaviour that he identifies himself with them because he has never bothered to observe their origin. There are other desires that are not of the body, but man, again, seldom pauses to observe these desires in himself.

But for us who are observers of ourselves there can never be a hidden desire or hidden motivation. If we are always observing ourselves nothing hidden can come in without being spotted and nothing hidden can get done because we, the master, are always there.

Motivation is the action of a desire and desire always produces its own energy for its fulfilment. The energy is produced by conflict and conflict is to want to change what is. You can desire to go to the cinema but the desire-energy-action does not begin until the moment you desire to change what is — now. What is only exists now. Tomorrow is what may be. Yesterday is what was. If you want to do anything there has to be a desire and as soon as the desire arises in your consciousness it exists and you can see it, you can observe it for yourself because it is then yourself.

Unconscious and subconscious have no place in the science of self-discovery except to spur us on. They can only mean there is something about ourselves we do not know, and that is intolerable. What is unknown might contain our freedom or immortality.

You touch a hot iron. You withdraw your hand instantly; there was no thought or decision in the reaction. The body's desire was to protect itself so it withdrew from the abnormal heat which would injure or destroy it.

It is the same with abnormal cold. Sometimes when the hand sticks to something abnormally cold like the bottom of a refrigerator tray the mind is not at first sure whether the sensation is heat or coldburn. Both sensations are the same to the body. All it does is withdraw instantly from that which would destroy it. Heat and cold have no distinction: the desire for preservation is the motivator. The body acts, performs, without your assistance — or rather without your thought or desire. In fact, if you try by thought to regulate the breath it becomes irregular.

When the body smells toxic fumes in the air it uses its mobility to escape. If it did not have a sense of smell it might be destroyed. In the same way taste and other senses are a defence system — they are self-preservation senses. The animals seem to act in the same way although they do not seem to try to interfere by thinking.

It is man's habit to see things in relation to his interests. If you see a snake and you perceive it in relation to self-preservation you will fail to see it as it is. You will not see the superb artistry of its skin pattern, the cold yet vibrant lustre, the wonder of its coiling movements, the brightness of its eyes, the nervous movement of its fine forked tongue. A snake is a thing of beauty if you look at it in relation to itself after reason has satisfied the desire for body protection. Beauty is not an interest — beauty is — and beauty is in all created things if you can put aside your interests and see them as they are. How else do you think you see beauty on the few occasions you do in your busy thought-full days? If beauty was not you could not spare the time to manufacture it and there would be no beauty. Beauty is despite you.

You are off to a business appointment. You take a short cut through the park. Your interest at the moment is in the appointment so you see the trees and flowers only in relation to the appointment — and are careful not to walk into the trees or trip over the bushes and flowers.

Compared to the trees our bodies possess mobility and the senses of seeing and hearing which trees apparently do not. But as above, so below, is one of the pivotal facts of the science of self-knowledge. A tree will send its roots very deep, even under a road if necessary, to find food or sustenance. It has the desire for food and because of that it lives or is. If there is waste oil the roots will avoid the place and if you keep chopping at a root it will go in another direction. When you wound a tree the sap congeals protectively around the wound, like blood. From this you can see that the tree combines elementary states of the senses of smell, taste, and touch-feeling. It would appear from the facts in our experience that the senses of smell, taste and touch-feeling are primarily associated with the desire of an organism — a body or plant — to preserve itself.

The tree does not apparently see or hear but the animals do and the result is a natural movement towards leadership or dominance by the fittest. This is where you come in, where man begins. The senses of seeing and hearing are the beginning of the desire for power apart from the desire for preservation of the organism and species. The desire for power for power's sake is the beginning of the individual existence — the robotman.

Without knowledge we are nothing:
nothing we can understand now.

POWER

What is it that drives you on to use the knowledge in your memory? What makes you strive so hard, and why do you keep going when you are already under sentence of death?

Your memory is filled with uncountable experiences, a teeming jumble of unconnected matters right back to childhood. Yet when something comes up for discussion only the absolutely relevant details present themselves to consciousness and you express them.

You meet a person you have not seen for twenty years. In the second it takes to shake his hand you recall his name and most of the things you know about him and experienced together. This surely is a miracle. Perhaps we have never observed it because we are always too busy, too thought-full looking for the miraculous.

This miracle is what I call the unifying principle of individual experience in this life. You have probably heard it termed the ego, but let us look at this amazing unifying principle of your experience. A principle is a fundamental element that can be demonstrated but not defined. Unifying means reducing to unity, which in time means continuity. This principle unifies all your individual experience of life into one amazing, intelligible, continuous expression which is you.

You are an expression of the desire for power. You devote your life to this desire. All your ambitions, all your strivings, are directed at satisfying it. When you imagine you achieve it you are happy, when you fail you are unhappy.

The body does not desire power. It only wants to be at ease, and ease includes exercise when it desires it. The body does not want company, it needs food, water, air and a few other simple things to keep it at ease. If it itches it will scratch itself without any decision by you, even when you are asleep.

If you doubt that the pursuit of power occupies almost all of your life you must ask yourself what causes you the greatest worry and anguish in your life. You will find it is the anticipated loss of power as position, possessions, prestige and permanence — in other words, the loss of your power as an individual, which is death. The loss of a loved one can cause anguish but it will not interfere for long with the pursuit of power.

Your motives for pursuing power as all these things are secondary and in fact are imaginary. The pursuit is the fact. The motives are the excuses for the unending pursuit you cannot explain. For the youth the motive — applauded by all — is the desire to meet the challenge, to pursue fame and fortune. When he is a man and gets responsibilities he pursues exactly the same things, but now it is his duty. Now and again there is the exciting challenge and he forgets his excuses or motives of duty and pursues success or power with zest, but always the movement inside is back, back to where he started. A sort of weariness begins to show through but this has to be quickly covered up.

In middle age the motive becomes security or something like it. In old age, when the pursuit is old and has lost its vigour but not its virulence, the moments are more frequent when a person asks himself "What is it all about? What did I gain?". But it is too late, for soon he or she will die and anything gained will be taken. The pursuit never varies but the motives, the reasons, the excuses are endless.

To enjoy power you have to see it exist in relation to yourself, the powerful, and someone else, the powerless or the impressed.

Your desire for power is partly fulfilled when someone praises you, honours you, obeys you, serves you, works for you, quotes you, borrows from you or listens to you.

You are also more powerful in your imagination than another when you can tell him something he does not know, when you are first to break the news, when you discuss in someone's absence their failings or excesses, especially in relation to your own morality and respectability.

It is no use having a fortune in gold if you are alone on a desert island. Gold or money is only valuable for what it will buy, which includes respect. If you inherited an island teeming with people and wealth but you were born deaf and blind you would get no elation of power, no feeling of success. If you possess you have to see your possessions or the power-producing effect of them. If you rule you have to see or hear the power of your authority. The key is imagination.

The senses of seeing and hearing mark the beginning of what we term intelligence, which in man includes the faculties of reason and imagination. Without the senses of seeing and hearing imagination is almost totally absent, and without imagination there is no desire for power. For you can only desire what you can imagine. It is only by reason — the power to assemble facts in cogent form — that man can overcome the falseness of imagination. But it is so difficult and the forces of imagination are so powerful that few individuals ever succeed.

Both imagination and reason are activities of the ego — the unifying principle of your experience in this life. The imaginative aspect of the ego is that every desire is pursued with the feeling, the conviction, that you are permanent, that "it cannot happen" to you. But it will happen to you. There is no more obvious a fact than death, but it makes no difference. Reason is a babe against this giant of imagination that keeps the poor, shuffling, robot world in chains. You imagine from moment to moment that you are permanent. You are identifying yourself with the desire. But it is the desire that is permanent — not you.

When you are forced to look at death in relation to yourself you fear death. The operating surgeon does not feel this fear as he is looking at death in relation to another. But he, too, fears death when he is forced by circumstances to face the fact of death in relation to himself. Yet it is not death you both fear because you do not know what death compromises and you cannot fear what you do not know. You fear death because you know in your own experience it will take all your power, position, prestige, possess-ions — everything you imagine you are.

You will be alone when you find the secret of life; and you will be alone when you find the secret of death.

THE EDGE OF YOURSELF

Fear is not a fact. It is an assumption. It exists only in imagination and it is your constant companion and merciless whip. You are afraid when you think you will lose your life, power or possessions, but not in the moment of losing them. The most pressing and ever-present of these fears is the fear of what people will say. You are always in fear thinking, imagining, before the moment of action. No-one ever knows fear when aware and not thinking.

If during a war your imagined fear of going into combat is momentarily greater than the fear of what people will say if you do not you will not respond when the signal comes. The army knows from experience that something can happen to a man with time to think so its training and discipline are aimed at making him obey instantly without thought.

The body does not know fear, only the desire for self-preservation at the moment of threat, and then it acts within its limited capabilities. But you, the unifying principle which is the memory, the monitor of the senses plus the faculty of reason, use all these powers to protect the body before the moment of danger occurs. The problem is that as soon as this chattering chimpanzee of a mind sees or hears something it plunges into the jungle of associated ideas that are limitless in number in your memory. If you have one matter that is causing you concern, the mind will use every association to bring you back to it. It will suggest unending possibilities, most of them unfavourable or bad for you because you are concerned or upset and expecting the worst. This is the ceaseless agony of worry.

If the desire for power, position, possessions and permanence disappears your body will not die. All that will die is your fear. But only you can find out what remains when fear and desire have gone — and you will find out at the same time whether Christ and the rest of the prophets were fools.

If God exists God can be experienced, but only by you. If all the prophets swore on a stack of bibles — as they have — that God exists, you are no closer to experiencing God.

If you have found God through worship in a church or temple, through ritual and ceremony, through the teachings of a religious order, then that is good. But if you do not know whether God exists and you have a yearning you cannot explain, let us try to discover the truth together.

You know you exist because at any moment you can experience it. If anyone tells you they have seen a ghost, no matter how much you want to believe in the existence of ghosts you will not really accept it as a fact until you see the ghost with your own eyes, that is until you experience it.

The other way we accept things is by reason. We live our lives in a reasonable acceptance that the milkman will come, that the train will arrive, that we will be alive tomorrow to carry out today's planning. But the milkman might not come, we might die. These things are unlikely and reason will tell you so, but they do happen, every minute, somewhere. Reasonable acceptance has to ignore the unlikely. So, as you will have seen, not many people see or understand the presence of this element of the unlikely in living; most, obviously, do not or the unexpected would not shock. Reasonable acceptance, which is our living, is imperfect.

Reason is a mighty faculty but it is still below the state of awareness, of pure experiencing, which is the state you are in when you know "I exist" or "I am".

The fact is that unless you experience something for yourself it does not exist for you. Anything else exists in imagination first and then within reasonable acceptance. Imagination is unreliable and reasonable acceptance is imperfect. If God exists you must have the experience of it in the moment; otherwise you are absent and God cannot exist for you.

To go beyond reason we will have to use reason, like a ladder of reason climbing to the top of itself. That will not upset reason as reason is interested only in assembling the facts, whatever they might be. It is an ever-loyal tool, imagination without reason an ever-failing fool.

At the top of reason is awareness and pure experience — the edge of yourself, and possibly the beginning of God. Imagination has been left down below a long time ago. Reason begins where imagination ends. So to go to the edge of yourself you will first have to discard every idea, every image, everything you have ever read or been taught or heard about God.

To begin with, God is not good as you know good. If you think God is good it is imagination — you are deluding yourself.

There can be no lasting happiness in imperfection and perfection in the world is obviously not the object. If the creator wanted the world to be perfect for us it would be perfect. So happiness is not the creator's object as you may have noticed. In relation to the creator there can be no accidents within the creation or it is not the creator's creation. God the creator if he exists is the creator of murder, suicide, disease, insanity, torture and devastation. God destroys the innocent child, the humble saint, the loving husband, the devoted son and daughter, the wise and good leader. At the same time God allows the murderer, the cruel, the merciless, the exploiter, all the so-called evil ones to live. So God is not good as you know good.

Whatever is good must surely depend upon the aim. But you do not know the creator's aim, so you do not know what is good.

If you are fighting a war anything that helps you win is good, any setback is bad. Do not men of "God" on either side ask God to bless his own creation by doing good for them which is bad for the other side and bad for the other side which is good at the same time? Such is the stupidity of the imagination. Robot man's good and bad must forever follow this crazy pattern of inconsistency while he imagines the object of his life to be separate from the object of all of life, the entire creation. What is good from the creator's standpoint must be what is good for the entire creation and every individual thing must exist to contribute towards the overall object irrespective of its personal idea of good. What is, is best. And if God does not exist — if there is no overall purpose and no overall good in relation to the entire creation — it does not matter anyway.

Many mystics have said, and it is true, that anything you see is not God. Anything you think is not God, neither are visions, lights, moving objects or anything else. Any sensation or feeling is not God. They are all the products of the creation or your imagination.

You may have visions and psychic experiences and you will be excited about them. You will think you are making progress — but it will be down the hill if you busy yourself with them. You will have taken a false trail made by the creation or imagination. If you experience the creator you can be sure there will be no room for doubts.

There are plenty of people and books that will tell you about psychic experiences. The experiences do exist as part of the creation. If you want to talk about them you will never be short of listeners or advisers, but God is way beyond them and God is our object.

The creator has to be experienced beyond the five senses and the only instrument that can experience in this way for you is yourself — in the state of thoughtless awareness in which you declare "I am" and hold it.

In the beginning the entire creation will seem to hinder, obstruct and try to keep you away from experiencing the creator. It is the way of things that only the unrelenting, the indomitable individual can escape and experience God. The curious masses always fail, but later on all things help, not hinder, the valiant.

On the way to God you will have to pass through beauty, pure beauty, and if you do not pass through beauty it is not God you have found. Beauty stands at the gate of the kingdom of heaven. It is of the creator, but not the creator, and it is all-mighty. Beauty is the only uncreated thing you can experience apart from God.

You experience beauty when you look at a sunset, the sea or the forest and an indescribable thing happens within your whole being for the briefest of moments. Then it is gone, and no matter how much and for how long you continue to look at that beautiful thing beauty does not return. But you can turn away and without thinking suddenly look again and beauty will strike your deepest note — and be gone again.

Beauty is and always is, but where are you? You, not beauty, are absent. Why are you absent? What keeps you from this indescribable ecstasy, this love, this truth, this peace? It must always be there because others experience it just as fleetingly while you do not.

Your robot mind is again the problem. It will not stay still and you cannot make it stay still. It is your master and it separates you from beauty and God. Beauty is experienced only from moment to moment. It cannot be held in memory and it cannot be willed. You can also only experience awareness, the highest state, from moment to moment, when there is no object, no reason, no action, no mind. So to experience beauty, love, truth and peace or God your mind has to be stilled.

While you seek anything before stillness you seek in vain. Stillness is the way.

BEYOND REASON

You spend most of your private life imagining — wishing, worrying and building on impressions. You can be ninety per cent certain that when you use the words 'if' and 'should' you are about to enter imagination.

Imagination is where you build on what someone told you about someone, where you impute motives, infer insult, and where you speculate about what a person meant by the inflexion of their voice.

Imagination is mostly desire without object or action and without the intention to act. When you do act on imagination you act on impulse and nearly always fall flat on your face. You experience this mostly in personal relationships.

Planning is reason with an object and the intention to act. Reason presents the facts but there is no action — yet. There is a reasonable acceptance, but go beyond reasonable acceptance and you drop into imagination. This is the line between the intelligent and the unintelligent person in the world; between the sought-after man with his feet on the ground and the fool with his impractical schemes who worries himself into ill-health and calls it nerves.

Thinking is mistaking impressions for facts. Reason does not need thinking. If you observe yourself in the state of planning you will notice that having fixed the object the facts just keep coming, linking up into a chain of proposed action. But when you are in the state of imagination, beyond reasonable acceptance and building on impressions, you will notice you build outwards, away from yourself. Worry has no object; you only imagine it has. The process is most dissatisfying and you know it is stupid even while it is going on.

The beginning of awareness, or experiencing from moment to moment, is reason with object and action. But reason acts quickly in awareness — a thousand times faster than thought — and you do not even notice it is operating. Driving a car is an example of this.

You are always in the state of awareness when you love what you are doing. You are aware all the time for love keeps you awake and in union with the action. You are also creative in this state, but the state of awareness diminishes as you get used to the job — and you go back to sleep.

If you attain your object the moment of attainment cannot be held. The moment is part of the creation so it is in time and it must die as everything in the creation must die, so that the next moment can be born. The moment is the last created thing in relation to you.

The state of awareness lasts as long as the action. When the action is over you begin thinking and are out of the state of meditation, which is what awareness is.

A further state of awareness is the beginning or edge of pure awareness. For purposes of description it is awareness with reason, without action but with an object. The object is the state itself and it disappears with the experiencing of the state. You are in this state at the moment you experience that you exist, that I am.

To experience you exist the mind is momentarily stopped. You draw all your faculties into yourself, you meditate on the moment and you experience I am. But only for a moment. You are still in time, and still in the creation, so the moment of attainment must die.

At the moment I am there is no reason, no object, no action — just I am. If you could hold the state even the I am would disappear and you would be in the silence on the edge of time. For this split second you are at the apex of consciousness; just beyond is where God, the timeless or the uncreated begins. The moment, as we have seen, is the last thing created.

But to begin with you can remain there only long enough to experience I am. You can repeat the experience but it will still last less than a moment and be gone. You cannot hold this state in the present, wandering, ever-desiring condition of your mind. If you think you can, look again. You are imagining it and you will see you are in a state of no apparent thought but you are not aware of your environment. It is like when you stare into space: you are not aware, you are absent, you are unconscious of your existence. You can only get next to God with the effort of preparation.

To begin experiencing the uncreated, the state that begins with I am will have to be held for several minutes. If it can be held for minutes it can be held for hours, and if it can be held for hours it can be held continuously. You are then between time and the timeless waiting for the unknown which will come but cannot be willed. You will then understand why a man once said "I am in this world but not of it". It is here that you can eventually realise not only "I am" but "I am God".

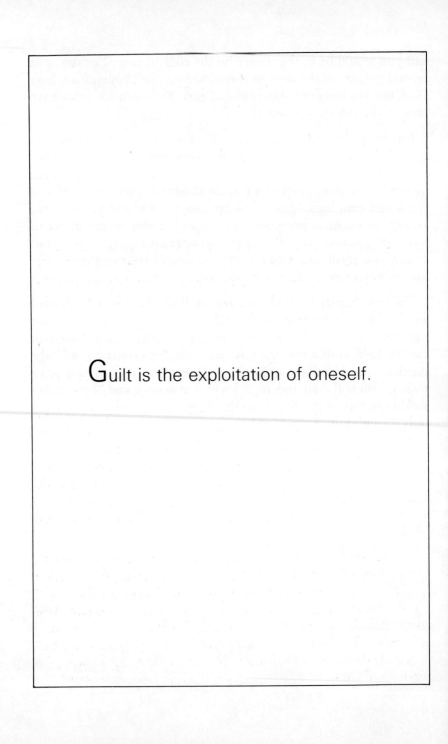

Guilt is the exploitation of oneself.

HONESTY

Faith is knowledge. The reason people think it is something else is because they are superficial and live on the sandbank of themselves. If they ever pause to peer into the deep, crystal water around them they rarely penetrate beyond the dancing illusion of the sunlight on the surface.

You use faith all the time. It is your faith in the world that gets you through each busy day. But the trouble with worldly faith is that it is subject to error and the Mars element. Real faith is knowledge of yourself.

"Have faith", the preachers cry. You might as well cry "Be hungry" to a man with a full stomach, or "Be happy" to the man whose heart is heavy with sorrow. The fact is you cannot tell anyone to have faith. If you do not have faith that means the concepts of other minds are unacceptable to you, and so they should be. You cannot learn truth, you have to discover it — experience it. So your non-faith or agnosticism is only the rejection of canned ideas.

All knowledge, all faith, is within you now, at this moment. That is why I have said you must not believe me. If you go inside yourself, know yourself by observation and awareness, you will know the truth of this and the truth will set you free of doubt. You cannot be told any wisdom, any truth, that is not already waiting to be discovered just below the surface of what you call your conscious mind. A word of truth, an illustration of truth, can bring the dormant knowledge to the surface. People can recite words of great wisdom with drama and never understand them, for the words have to match what they have discovered within.

The only test of what you know or believe is what you live by acting on. Anything else is imagination. The world is full of "I believers" and they really believe they believe. The professional "I believers" — the politicians, the broadcasters, the newspaper pundits — know they are liars and poseurs. But what about the others? If you pin an "I believer" with an inquiry to discover whether he lives it and he does not he will equivocate, make excuses and lie again, or if trapped he will indignantly declare "I know what I believe".

You have two honesties. The one you believe in and the one you live. You cannot adhere to the code you profess because your honesty changes with nearly every challenge. But because you are unconscious of this fact you excuse your inconstancy by a "justified in the circumstances" explanation — another expression for dishonesty.

There is no truth for the man-machine in a code that says you shall not kill, you shall not cheat, you shall not lie — beautiful as it might sound. It is a static thing in a world of ever-moving desires, a denial of the fact of man's life. There is a permanent unchanging honesty but you cannot understand it until you rise above the machine that asserts "I believe" and does not live it.

You lie to hide the person you really are so that you will be liked or respected, or to give yourself the appearance of having more power or prestige than in fact you have; and also to give yourself the appearance of being more honest than you are. If a stranger came up to you and told you you are a liar, you cheat, deceive, hold bad will, are unkind and cruel and cannot control your passions you would probably defend yourself vigorously. If he kept probing, you would probably lie and make excuses — all because you profess a code of honesty you do not live. Because everyone does it everyone expects it, and eventually the lie becomes the way of life.

Your strongest desires dictate what you do. They are the key that winds you up like a toy rooster that struts around for a few minutes imagining it is doing what it wants to and at the same time imagining it is being honest because it obeys the mechanical law which is its very existence.

You may say you do things you do not desire to do, but that is an example of imagination and lack of self-knowledge. While you desire to exist, you have to put up with all that that desiring involves.

Can you change your desire for money so that it is gone and never returns? Or your desire for power or prestige which you are pursuing so vigorously? You cannot. What would you change it to anyway? To the desire to be honest all the time? You can of course say you do not want to change, which means you do not desire to, which means you desire the desires you are already pursuing. You cannot change while you desire.

If you renounce anything you renounce nothing. Renunciation is a reaction of desire and a part of the original desire itself. By renouncing something all you do is change the direction of your desiring and continue with the same drive as before.

Your basic driving desire for power can never be fulfilled. But it can cease to exist when you experience most of what power stands for, and see with an indescribable realisation that it is nothing, that what you have always been chasing is just a road to nowhere.

Where there is desire there is no freedom.

WILLPOWER

A man falls overboard from a ship into a cold ocean and swims around all night before he is picked up. It is incredible how he was able to keep going. Willpower? No. Desirepower. His desire to survive was stronger than his desire to give up.

A businessman loses everything in a financial crash, begins again, working fourteen hours a day seven days a week, and in three years rebuilds his business. Willpower? No. Desirepower. His desire to be a success or to possess money and power was stronger than his desire to be a good family man or husband or anything else.

A fat woman known for her gluttony goes on a diet and in three months reduces to trim proportions. Willpower? No. Desirepower. Her desire not to be fat was stronger than her desire for food.

Desirepower is easily identified because you will always imagine that by using it you stand to gain something. The greater the desirepower, the greater the effort or sacrifice. But because desires vary with every individual and because ways of achieving these desires also vary, one person may display tremendous desirepower where another does not.

You will notice that you do not use the expression willpower when a person saves another's life. You say he was brave or fearless. If he does it without thinking it is an act of love, but if he thinks before he acts it is because he imagines there is something in it for him, even if it is only that his desire not to be called a coward is stronger than his desire not to go to the rescue. A man who thinks never goes to certain death to save another. If he does go he thinks he will make it.

There is nothing wrong with desirepower for it is life itself. But desirepower is not willpower.

Man's development from a machine into a conscious man depends upon his discovering and understanding the principles of willpower and love. Understanding of willpower leads to the understanding of the principle of love.

Willpower is equilibrium, the absence of desire or reaction. Anything equalised is in balance, at rest. Will is the power that overcomes desire.

Life is held together by willpower. Desire can be said to manifest in all living things and to reach a peak of expression in man, but it fails utterly to effect the equilibrium of what is. Every single thing that desires dies, is inevitably annihilated. And life goes on, untouched and serene. Whatever it is that holds life together has obviously overcome desire.

The results of desirepower are tangible and enviable; but you will not be seen to be gaining anything desirable from applying willpower. There is nothing at all in it for the robot man.

Willpower can be exercised only in yourself. It cannot be inflicted on anyone or anything outside — not even on your own body. If you try this you will be using desirepower.

Willpower is an energy — the finest and most combustible energy in the human organism and the first energy to be destroyed in anger and other emotional reactions. You tap into willpower — and start overcoming desire — when you observe yourself getting angry or impatient and can smile and let go of the emotion, die to it, because you see the futility of it.

Willpower does not mean suppression — suppression being merely a reaction of desire. Being able to use willpower depends first on your alertness in being present when the emotion is actually rising in you. Secondly, it depends on your ability to counterbalance the emotion by immediately understanding the false claim it is imposing on you — that it is you.

No desire is individual. The desire of the body for food is the desire of all bodies, which means the desire itself is not individual. But you will insist on associating individuality with pursuit of the common desire for power, possessions, position or prestige.

Desire is the stamp of the herd, the unconscious mass. Only the instant understanding of the false claim it is making on you as an individual can enable you to cut off from it and be free of it without frustration.

You can assume for the purpose of discovering willpower that virtually everyone you know except yourself is moving in an eternal mechanical circle and believes with a conviction as strong as life itself that it is the only practical way to live. You either go with them, or you go against them — but they will feel it. No willpower is needed to go with them, just desirepower, and not much of that. Anyone who falters will be dragged along.

Everyone has desirepower and buried under it is willpower. But until you have started to realise the pain and futility of living as desire, willpower remains hidden and involuntary.

Usually the first sign that it is beginning to show through is when a person pauses, stands back for a few moments from his identification with his busy world, and sighs "Where am I going? What is it all about?". If this occurs in the midst of sorrow caused by frustration, disappointment or loss, nothing is likely to come of it. But if it occurs at all sorts of times, especially in moments of success and gain, the person is ready.

The next sign is when you see you are not free and that you, and you alone, are to blame.

That is as far as that first bit of willpower will take you; the rest, the escape, is up to you.

Love does not leave men and women;
men and women leave love.

UNION

Why is it that you do not really love — and you know it? Why is it that so often you have to pretend to love those you love?

Love is giving of yourself. Your possessions are not of yourself so to give those is not love. Your house, food, money are not of yourself so to give those is not love. If you have lots of money you can give lots of things, but if you have no money you can give none. The homeless and the pauper must be able to love too.

If you give advice, that is of your experience. If you give your opinions that is of your pride. If you say "I love you" that is of your breath. If you work for others, feed them, house them, educate them, you work for yourself first. If you give of your time you must take it from something else and taking can never come into giving.

You just give your love, you say? No you do not. The hen and the sow do as much for their own. You have no love to give and that is why you know you do not love. Yet you can love . . . but only in the moment.

Love is ever moving like everything else, and yet it is constant. Man imagines he contains love and makes a static thing of it like honesty, then he is shocked when he sees he does not love. This makes him lie to those he "loves", and worse, to himself.

Man's love is desire. To desire is to want to receive. Man imagines his love is something he gives but this cannot be.

When a man loves a woman, or vice versa, it is expressed as the desire to be with her, to live with her. His desire will give him no peace until they are together and he imagines that as soon as they are together it will be the fulfilment of his desire. Despite his later denials he imagines that the fulfilment will carry with it a continuing state of happiness, contentment. Otherwise he would not love or desire her. But a desire is to want to receive and this means he is taking or receiving, not giving. So is she, for she desires him as he desires her, and she too is receiving not giving.

They are both receiving the beautiful feeling of love. Where is it coming from? Love itself is giving.

Love is a power, a mighty principle that exists in its own right independent of any individual. Man changes but the principle of love does not and cannot. Love does not leave men and women — men and women leave love.

Man's desire for his loved one is doomed to disappear in the very delight of its fulfilment. The desire to be with, the desire to know the other, to experience everything about the other, is the basis of man's and woman's love. But when you know everything about anything you contain it, are one with it, and begin to lose interest in it. So to continue to desire another with the same freshness as when you first fell in love, the beloved will have to have a quality of timelessness, of unknowableness.

Whenever you desire anything, you desire knowledge. This is because you cannot add anything to yourself except knowledge. It does not matter what you possess or gain, you cannot add it to yourself. All you add is the knowledge that you possess it and can experience it or use it at any time. This knowledge is the fulfilment of the desire for the object.

Your body needs air. You desire the knowledge that the air is there. Once you have that knowledge the desire, for you, is fulfilled. Otherwise you would worry and try to organise a continual supply of air for the future.

You desire to read a book. You do not desire the book as an object. If you do you want only the knowledge that the book is in your possession for you to experience at any time. If your desire is fulfilled you do not read the book again, the knowledge is already yours and there is no desire.

You desire power. The only way you know your desire is being fulfilled is by seeing or hearing others obeying you. If you were in a prison cell and kept sending out orders without knowing they were being obeyed, your desire for power would not be fulfilled and you would probably be called mad.

The fact of human love is that man or woman desires to live with the loved one so that he or she can absorb the other entirely, possess them by knowing everything about them. This desire contains its own destruction.

The period of fulfilment, of knowing each other, does not usually last very long because there is not much to know and not much worth knowing in men and women unless they love God or the truth. Truth and God are depthless and timeless and those who love them develop the same qualities. Usually what you get to know is mostly personality and personality is an act. You cannot act all the time and as each sees the truth of what the other is the masks are left off more and more. The masks are gaily trotted out with full paintwork for others to see; but there is little mystique between the former lovers. The partnership is mechanical and predictable.

To begin with, love is longing, the separation of a desire from its fulfilment plus the brief period of fulfilment. Then it is sex, expectation, fear, compatibility, familiarity and habit. The union usually results in a kind of oneness if the desires or interests of the two are similar. If most desires can be fulfilled as a partnership reasonable peace remains. If they cannot there is conflict.

Love is all around you like the air and is the very breath of your being but you cannot know it, feel its unfeeling touch, until you pause in your busy-ness and are still and poised and empty of your wanting and desiring. When at rest the air is easily offended and will flee even from the fanning of a leaf, as love flees from the first thought. But when the air or love moves of its own accord it is a hurricane that drives all before it.

The understanding of love comes with the knowledge that you are nothing. The greatest purity is nothing or nothingness — no thinking, no desiring, no imagining. You are then one with the moment and the great movement of life so nothing can happen that is not right. Every moment is perfect and everything that happens is eternally just.

Doubt is thought.

WAR AND STRIFE

The eternal law of magnetism is that opposite attracts opposite and like repels like. In the electrical circuit the flow is the same: connect positive to positive or negative to negative and nothing happens.

Yet in the world of man, or the world of man's mind, like attracts like and opposites repel. How can there be two contradictory laws?

Man's world is the world of his mind. His mind is the source of his personality, ambition, like and dislike, good and bad. In everything man is either for or against. He says there are two sides to every question but what he says is not true: there can only be two sides if personal interests, which means selfish interests, are involved. Otherwise something is either true or false, or the facts available at the time are insufficient to allow a conclusion to be reached.

If two people want to establish whether an animal is a cow they look at it and say, "Yes, this is a cow". There are only the facts of what a cow is. There are no selfish interests or opinions — man's most treasured possessions.

But if one of the people says it is his cow and the other says it is not, there is a difference of opinion. They are now in the world of mind where like attracts like and opposites repel.

The Hindus will tell you the cow is sacred. That is their treasured opinion and there are several hundred million of them. You may disagree. It is a case of for and against, a matter of opinion; but not a matter of fact because no mind knows.

In the mind-world opinions and beliefs are more important than facts. So there is little hope of agreement in this world: issues invariably polarise into two opposing sides of opinions and beliefs.

But the fact is that both sides are wrong: the argument in favour could not exist without the argument against. Remove the arguments and there is no dispute. What remains is the fact — and you cannot argue over a fact. Factions arise from looking at the argument instead of looking for the fact.

If the two factions go to war it is to prove nothing but the force of their respective arguments — while the fact of the matter is left ignored and undiscovered.

By the time the factions finish fighting, the fact they failed to see at the outset is not only still not visible but probably no longer apposite. Every fact has its moment — and the moment and the fact have moved on.

No disagreement can be resolved except by action. Nothing is ever resolved except by action. Then which side had the stronger means of argument — not which was correct — becomes the fact, if it matters. If you have the power you have your way.

Do you see a pattern? Where have man's opinions been taking him since the beginning of history? Where are your opinions taking you? Nowhere — except towards useless conflict. There is nowhere else to go. All that life demands of you while you remain mechanical is that you keep busy doing nothing so that its greater purpose beyond your busy imagination can be eternally served.

The eternal law as opposed to the law of man's mind is that heat attracts cold and cold attracts heat — until a balance or equilibrium is reached. This balance extends between the limits of heat and cold needed to support life on earth — somewhere between the cold of the poles and the hottest place on earth.

Similarly, light attracts dark and dark attracts light until a balance is reached. If there was no dark in the light we would be blinded, and if there was no light in the dark something equally damaging and incompatible would happen.

You will notice that this attraction of opposites, each tending to cancel the other out, is a process of de-creation; but that it always stops arbitrarily at the point of balance needed to support life. If it were allowed to continue past that point, the opposites would eventually unite like desire and its fulfilment and the creation would disappear. Nothing would remain except the state that existed before the creation began.

The precise opposite to this process is man's self-centred creation, his world in which like forces attract like — like attracts like and hate attracts hate. This world is an attempt to create within the creation itself by a clumsy sort of reverse process. It is self-propagating instead of self-cancelling, divisive instead of unifying. If man had his way, the likes on the one side and the likes on the other side would continue to enlarge and spread until the whole world condensed into two immovable blocks of intractable opinion.

But man does not have his way: war and fighting see to that. In man's self-centred, self-conscious world, war and strife are necessary equivalents of the violent function of nature in the natural world: they are life's way of breaking down the monoliths and providing the breathing space for them to breed again.

As nature through the law of opposites uses violence and destruction to preserve and replenish itself in perfect harmony, so the discordant man-made world depends on war and strife to preserve itself in perfect disharmony.

I have seen what virtue is and it is the
death of me.

DIVIDE AND DIE

There is an eternal law that can guide man. It will never leave him in doubt about what he should do. It contains no room for extenuating circumstances, justifications or changing values of the kind that snarl up man-made and mind-made laws. It is a law that the innocent bewildered part of man can understand. And even though he may infringe it he can see for himself at every turn of the way the unerring signpost of eternal justice.

The law is: Divide and die.

It does not refer to physical division but to the mental fences we erect that divide us from the world on one side and our being on the other. We live in a narrow no-man's land of fences.

You feel your being, or you are your being, when you know those brief moments of love and when you experience the happiest and most ecstatic moments of your life that are not the result of the fulfilling of any desire you can name. It is your being that knows beauty, it is your being that knows love and your being is your conscious self. Your non-conscious self is your mind and it cannot experience any of these things nor can it know your being. But when the mind is still and innocent of desire it becomes transparent and you become your being that shines through like a thousand suns. You feel divine . . . and you are.

Your being unites, your mind divides. Only by division does the individual robot grow. Division is a death of your being and life to your mind. Union is death to your mind and life to your being — and this is the state of immortality.

When you smile and mean it at the moment of giving of yourself, your being reaches out and unites with the object of your smile. It might be two birds playing on a branch or a child trying to stand up. In smiling you have added the object to your being and yet you have given of yourself. You have become bigger and yet you have become smaller. It is your being, your beautiful self, that has become bigger and your little divisive thinking self that has become smaller.

When you frown or scowl you divide yourself from the object or event. Instead of going out to it you step back from it. Your being, your beautiful self, shrinks and you, your mind, the judge, the divider, the individual robot, grow bigger. You have divided yourself from another and by the eternal law you must suffer.

The immediate penalty for breaking this law is unhappy feelings of irritation, anger, hatred, envy and bitterness. You don't suffer when you smile.

But this is an eternal law too and its justice is felt in the eternal world as well as in time. While you break this great law you separate yourself from immortality; for it is your being that is immortal and unless you are being your being you are not immortal. To divide yourself from your being is living death, and that is how man lives — in a sort of death which he treasures as life.

Do you see the superb justice of the great law? You do not really harm others with your scowl or curse, you harm yourself. This law is for the individual alone because only the individual can learn to be honest with himself. If he knows he has not divided by his word or action and yet all the world says he has done wrong, he is free. Only the individual can know if he has obeyed this great law, and if he has it is important only to him.

☆

Your being knows only two states. One is the state of neutrality or rest; the other is beauty.

The harmony of beauty is in being. When you walk into a room or look at anything and like it without thinking, it is beauty that has struck the same note of beauty in your being.

There are no opposites in being, there is no dislike — only neutrality and beauty. Neither requires judgement. They are a state — as immersion in water is a state — and you do not have to judge or think to experience it. Neither divides. Being either likes or loves — which without thought is beauty — or is neutral, and your life is spent in innocent indifference to most of the things around you.

Mind is busy all the time. It hates the state of neutrality or rest in itself without an occupying interest because then its mastery is threatened. When mind encounters this state it rushes for a book or the television or someone to talk to. To consciously reach being you have to resist the mind's constant demand for activity and endure the restlessness, loneliness and discontent. Mind's desperate measures to fill every moment keep you from being, your conscious immortal self.

If you would do good, or want to help, be careful you do not intrude. If you would outspeed the moment and chase a cause be sure you are prepared to die for it; otherwise you are intruding on yourself and dividing yourself from yourself. If you are invited by the appearance of the cause you are invited by the mind and you work first for yourself. The need of anything is known only to being and if you are that thing's need you will be united with it as help. You will have no choice, nor want one.

If you are with a person or in a place and feel disharmony, then go. There is no need to divide. Unite yourself with another place or person. If a man is foolish and you can show him quietly, even though vigorously, that he is foolish, then most will thank you and both of you will gain. If not, leave him in indifference. But if you call him a fool and try to give him your opinion, he must in return give you his and both of you will be right and both of your opinions will be wrong.

If you ever have to kill make sure it is not you who pulls the trigger or pushes the bomb button. Let the man-machine do that — and you remain conscious, watching from your being in the state of equilibrium. If you do kill only you will know whether you intruded, and if you did not intrude you, the robot, died a little with your victim.

You are not special: you may yet have to kill. If it were meant to be that the man-machine was not to kill there would be no killing. But if you would die before you kill you are indeed special — a sacrifice of life for itself.

You have two prides. The one you know is the one of your mind, your imagination, which you will vary or bury to satisfy a desire of the moment and resurrect when you imagine you are offended.

But your true pride is of being and it will never let you sink below what is your essential dignity. This pride is beyond knowing, but not beyond observing. It is of the moment and its power is truth and innocence. It is the dignity of life itself and life will defend that dignity — killing you to preserve it if necessary. When this pride rules, you will die for it willingly, fearlessly, with a smile on your lips. Not out of defiance, but out of compassion for those who would imagine they can separate you from your eternal dignity.

SELECT INDEX

*for details of Barry Long's other
publications and current teaching
write to*

*The Barry Long Foundation
BCM Box 876 London WC1N 3XX
England*

---

*The Barry Long Centre (Australia)
PO Box 46 Eagle Heights Qld 4271
Australia*